America The Beautiful

Julie Anne Savage
Lyrics by Katharine Lee Bates

America The Beautiful

Copyright © 2018 by Julie Anne Savage

Green Apple Lessons Inc. Publishing. All rights reserved. No part of this book may be reproduced or transmitted in any form or by any means without written permission from the author.

Credits: America The Beautiful lyrics by Katharine Lee Bates.

Images © Adobe Stock. Resale or use of any images from this book is strictly prohibited.

ISBN/SKU: 9780692122785

Katharine Lee Bates was a poet and English teacher. In 1893, she took a train trip from Massachusetts to Colorado Springs, Colorado, to teach summer school. On her long journey across the country, she was moved by the beauty and grandeur of America's landscapes. Along her journey, she noted the "amber waves of grain" while passing through the wheat fields of Kansas. She also stopped for a visit to the 1893 World's Fair in Chicago, where she admired the gleaming white buildings and architecture of the "alabaster city."

Once arriving in Colorado, Bates later took a prairie wagon expedition to the summit of Pike's Peak, the highest summit of the southern front range of the Rocky Mountains. Upon reaching the apex and looking down at the vast valleys below, she was again touched by God's glory and splendor revealed through nature. Bates' travel experiences served as the inspiration for her poem entitled "Pikes Peak." In 1910, her poem was set to music written by composer, Samuel Augustus Ward, and soon became one of our country's most beloved patriotic songs, *America The Beautiful*.

One day some of the other teachers and I decided to go on a trip to 14,000-foot Pike's Peak. We hired a prairie wagon. Near the top we had to leave the wagon and go the rest of the way on mules. I was very tired. But when I saw the view, I felt great joy. All the wonder of America seemed displayed there, with the sea-like expanse.

~ Katharine Lee Bates

O beautiful for spacious skies,

For amber waves of grain,

For purple mountain majesties

Above the fruited plain!

America! America!

God shed His grace on thee

And crown thy good with brotherhood

From sea to shining sea!

O beautiful for pilgrim feet,

Whose stern, impassioned stress

A thoroughfare for freedom beat

Across the wilderness!

America! America!

God mend thine every flaw,

Confirm thy soul in self-control,

Thy liberty in law!

O beautiful for heroes proved

In liberating strife,

Who more than self their country loved

And mercy more than life!

America! America!

May God thy gold refine,

Till all success be nobleness,

And every gain divine!

O beautiful for patriot dream

That sees beyond the years

Thine alabaster cities gleam

Undimmed by human tears!

America! America!

God shed His grace on thee

And crown thy good with brotherhood

From sea to shining sea!

www.ingramcontent.com/pod-product-compliance

Lightning Source LLC
Chambersburg PA
CBHW041326290426
44110CB00004B/147